# MONKEY!

Colin Teevan

# MONKEY!

A tale from China

OBERON BOOKS
LONDON

WWW.OBERONBOOKS.COM

First published in 2001 by Oberon Books Ltd.
521 Caledonian Road, London N7 9RH
Tel: +44 (0) 20 7607 3637 / Fax: +44 (0) 20 7607 3629
e-mail: info@oberonbooks.com
www.oberonbooks.com

Reprinted with corrections 2003.

Reprinted 2011, 2012

A catalogue record for this book is available from the British
Library.

PB ISBN: 978-1-84002-257-5
E ISBN: 978-1-84943-630-4

Cover illustration by David Bradshaw

Printed, bound and converted
by CPI Group (UK) Ltd, Croydon, CR0 4YY.

Visit www.oberonbooks.com to read more about all our books
and to buy them. You will also find features, author interviews and
news of any author events, and you can sign up for e-newsletters
so that you're always first to hear about our new releases.

You cannot travel on the path before you have become the path itself

*– Gautama Buddha*

for Oisín and Lily

# Preface

The stories of Sun Wu-k'ung, the Monkey of the Mind are probably best known in the Western world from the Japanese cult TV show *Monkey!* which aired in the late 1970s and early 1980s. Yet the stories of the magic Monkey King date back at least as far as the fifth century AD. Monkey appears in the Indian epic *Ramayana*, and many plays from the Yuan dynasty – Late Medieval China – feature the adventures of the stick-fighting simian on the road to enlightenment.

The most complete surviving retelling of his exploits, however, is the *Hsi-yu Chi* which was first published in 1592. The *Hsi-yu Chi* – or *The Journey to the West* in Anthony C. Yu's masterful four volume English version – tells how Monkey was banished from the heavens for eating the peaches of eternal life. After five hundred years locked in a mountain, he was released and, with the pig monster, Pigsy, and the sand-eel monster, Sandy, accompanied the monk Tripitaka, on a journey to the Western Heaven to fetch the scriptures of the laws from Tathagata Buddha. The bulk of the text is taken up with the foursome's eighty-one adventures on the road to the West. In its English form it weighs in at a scale-breaking 1900 pages!

Arthur Waley in his introduction to his massively bow-dlerised Penguin translation of *The Journey to the West*, entitled *Monkey*, describes it as a 'combination of beauty with absurdity, of profundity with nonsense'. While it is, at times, hilariously funny and the worlds presented might appear alien to Western readers, Waley misses the serious intentions behind the work and, by random editing, destroys the vast architecture of the piece. In fact, so seriously is this work treated in certain quarters in China that there are rituals of hand washing and prayer that must be performed before one may even read a single chapter. For what the author – now largely believed not to be the Wu Ch'eng-En to whom Waley ascribes the work

– seems to be intending, is the story of mankind; from the egotistical demands of the childish mind (Monkey) through an encounter with the soul (Tripitaka), the appetite (Pigsy) and the intuition (Sandy), to the full achievement of self.

Furthermore, the author of *The Journey to the West* was sponsored by the Ming Dynasty and there is also a political/religious agenda behind the book. This is nothing less than the attempt to reconcile the dichotomies between Great Wheel and Little Wheel Buddhism and Buddhism in general and Taoism. Tripitaka was a historical character in the T'ang Dynasty in the sixth century. He travelled to the source of Buddhism in the Hindu Kush to obtain core Buddhist texts in their original language so that the T'ang Emperor might unify competing religious factions in his Empire. By sponsoring the collation of the Monkey and Tripitaka stories, the Ming Emperor in the sixteenth century sought an instrument to unify the religions of his times.

All this might appear rather earnest stuff to base a family show upon. But it is the genius of the original author that he created in Monkey, Pigsy, Sandy and Tripitaka characters of such wit, humour, magic and empathy that one is endlessly amused by the scrapes they land themselves in and moved by their gradual progress towards enlightenment. As a group of characters they more resemble Dorothy and her travelling companions from The Wizard of Oz than anything from Classical Western mythology.

Colin Teevan
November 2001

# Characters

BUDDHA

MONKEY

YAMA KING OF DEATH

JADE EMPEROR

SPIRIT OF THE PLANET VENUS

ERH-LANG

PRIME MINISTER OF CHINA

EMPEROR T'AI TSANG OF CHINA

SOLDIERS OF THE IMPERIAL GUARD

TRIPITAKA

GENERAL YIN

YIN'S DEMONS

BOY

MR KAO

DAUGHTER NUMBER THREE

PIGSY

SANDY/FISH DRAGON*

MOTHER DEMON/LITTLE OLD MAN/LITTLE OLD
WOMAN/PRIEST*

WILY WORM/SICKLY SON/DEAF DAUGHTER/ DISAP-
POINTING DISCIPLE*

SLY DEVIL/SICKLY SON/DEAF DAUGHTER/ DISAP-
POINTING DISCIPLE*

GHOST OF KING OF BLACK ROOSTER/TRUE KING OF
BLACK ROOSTER*

PRINCE OF BLACK ROOSTER

QUEEN OF BLACK ROOSTER

FALSE KING OF BLACK ROOSTER/FALSE TRIPITAKA*

DEATHLY DEMONS

* The / indicates characters who transform in the course of their story.
Doubling-up of parts is up to the director of a particular production.

*Monkey!* was first performed at the Young Vic Theatre, London, on 22 November 2001 with the following cast:

MONKEY,  Elliot Levey

TRIPITAKA,  Inika Leigh Wright
PIGSY,  Jan Knightley
SANDY,  Jason Thorpe

Other parts played by: Aicha Kossoko, Don Klass, Sang Cam Lui, Andrew Wareham and Tom Wu


Director, Mick Gordon

Designer, Dick Bird
Lighting Designer, Neil Austin
Sound Designer, Crispian Covell
Music, Kila

# ACT ONE

*An empty stage.*

BUDDHA: In the beginning there was nothing
And nothing was everything;
The heavens, the air, the earth, the oceans and the under-
world
Were nowhere and everywhere;
For real form is that form which has no form
And Buddha's whole world is but a grain of sand
Where true fullness is emptiness.
But the earth, being restless as it is,
Coupled with the heavens, and they made an egg,
And out of this egg was born a monkey.
And this monkey was a special monkey
Because he was the first monkey of all monkeys:
Sun Wu-k'ung; the monkey of the mind.
And he was irrepressible.

*MONKEY is born.*

MONKEY: It's time to play.

*In a furious fight, MONKEY defeats a myriad demons
and monsters.*

I am Monkey, the Handsome Monkey King and I shall
live forever.

*YAMA KING OF DEATH is revealed.*

Who are you?

YAMA: I am Yama King of Death.

MONKEY: What do you want?

YAMA: Your number. It has come up.

MONKEY: And which number would that be?

YAMA: Soul number 1350. Here it is in my Book of Death. You are, or should I say were, Sun Wu-k'ung the Handsome Monkey King?

MONKEY: That is my name but it's not worn out yet. May I see your book?

YAMA: Certainly.

*YAMA passes book. MONKEY looks at the book and erases his name.*

MONKEY: There.

YAMA: You've rubbed out your number, you've rubbed out the numbers of all your monkey friends, you outrageous orang-utan.

MONKEY: Now I shall live forever. So if you'll excuse me, Yama King of Death, I must return to Flower-fruit Mountain to have a rumpus.

YAMA: You can't do that. You can't treat death in this way. It's not right. It's not respectful. What would happen if everyone treated death in this way? What would happen if everyone lived forever? The Great Wheel would stop turning, there would be an end to enlightenment.

MONKEY: Enlightenment? What's enlightenment?

YAMA: I'll show you enlightenment you ignorant ape.

MONKEY: Looks like he wants to play!

*They fight. MONKEY tricks YAMA.*

I am Monkey, the Handsome Monkey King. I am the equal of heaven.

*MONKEY escapes.*

YAMA: Equal of heaven? I'll give you heaven. I'll go to the Jade Emperor of the Eastern Heaven.

*The Eastern Heaven. YAMA, the JADE EMPEROR and the SPIRIT OF THE PLANET VENUS have tea.*

JADE EMPEROR: Equal of heaven? My equal?

YAMA: I demand you punish him, or I shall have to take matters into my own hands.

JADE EMPEROR: Enough, enough. I have heard enough of this monkey. What is that awful rumpus?

ALL: The monkey.

JADE EMPEROR: This monkey goes too far. First he breaks the rules of life and death, then he disturbs me at my afternoon green tea time. It is quite insupportable. I shall have him spanked until his bottom is quite red.

SPIRIT OF THE PLANET VENUS: His bottom is quite red, Your Jadeness, he is a monkey.

JADE EMPEROR: Well then, how do you suggest I punish him, Spirit of the Planet Venus?

SPIRIT OF THE PLANET VENUS: He knows the secrets of the seventy-two transformations. He knows the mystic arts of the cloud trapeze, besides, he has a very big stick. Perhaps you would demonstrate your great benevolence as well as your superior wisdom, not by punishing him, but by indulging him. Give him some worthless position in heaven and let him call himself what he wants. For he is a proud monkey and will think it a great honour. He will be too busy strutting about, feeling important, to realise that his position is quite meaningless.

JADE EMPEROR: Perhaps you are right, Spirit of the Planet Venus. I don't care what he calls himself, so long as he calls himself it quietly.

YAMA: But I demand you punish him.

JADE EMPEROR: Enough. You have made my tea quite
cold with your complaining. This so-called Monkey
King, Equal of Heaven can look after my Peach Garden.
Is not to make him a fruit farmer punishment enough?

YAMA: Of course, Jade Emperor, let him be a fruit farmer
for the time being. But I'll get him in the end. He will
not make a monkey of Yama King of Death.

*A heavenly peach garden.*

SPIRIT OF THE PLANET VENUS: So that concludes
the tour of the Peach garden. Now, there is one thing
you must remember.

MONKEY: Must remember. Must remember. Yes?

SPIRIT OF THE PLANET VENUS: These are the
Emperor's peaches. The peaches of eternal life. Each
peach helps you live 9000 years. But if anyone is caught
stealing them, they will receive a punishment worse
than death.

MONKEY: Worse than death? That is bad.

SPIRIT OF THE PLANET VENUS: It's worse than bad.
So, whatever you do, don't eat the peaches. Repeat after
me: Don't eat the peaches.

MONKEY: Don't eat the peaches.

SPIRIT OF THE PLANET VENUS: Now, carry on with
your duties.

MONKEY: Yes, my duties.

*Exit SPIRIT OF THE PLANET VENUS.*

Heaven at last. And my very own peach garden. (*Pause.*)
Ahh! (*Pause.*) But what are my duties? What are you
meant to do in heaven all day? (*Pause.*) It's ever so nice,

14

but ever so boring. Now what's this that the Spirit of the Planet Venus said? That's it, the peaches. (*Pause.*) Don't eat them or do eat them? Of course, of course, silly old Monkey. (*To himself.*) Don't eat the peaches, don't eat the peaches, don't… (*Mesmerised.*) Live nine thousand years? Don't…eat the peaches, eat the peaches, must eat the peaches. The Jade Emperor wouldn't notice if I took one of his peaches, would he? No, of course not. (*Eats.*) Mmmm… After all, there are so many peaches and I… Mmmmm… So nice, I'll just have one more and… perhaps just one last…

*MONKEY eats five peaches. Enter the JADE EMPEROR and the SPIRIT OF THE PLANET VENUS.*

JADE EMPEROR: Where is the Master of the Peach Garden? There is to be a heavenly peach festival today and I see no peaches on my peach trees. Where is that damned monkey?

SPIRIT OF THE PLANET VENUS: There he is, Your Jadeness.

JADE EMPEROR: There he is indeed, but where are my peaches? Answer me that you treacherous chimp.

*MONKEY spits five peach stones at the JADE EMPEROR.*

SPIRIT OF THE PLANET VENUS: Perhaps this is a job for your nephew, Master of Illustrious Sagacity Erh-lang, who with his two bladed lance mauled the marauding monsters from the Mud Cake River. He will know how to deal with this malfeasant monkey. He lives in retirement as a humble fisherman in the Kuan Province.

JADE EMPEROR: Better still, Spirit of the Planet Venus: call for my nephew, Master of Illustrious Sagacity Erh-lang.

*Flower-fruit Mountain.*

ERH-LANG: Sun Wu-k'ung you old monkey, you want to come and play?

MONKEY: I always want to play, Master of Illustrious Sagacity Erh-lang.

ERH-LANG: And so we played. Erh-lang, the champion of heaven –

MONKEY: Against Monkey the scourge of the earth. Magic stick –

ERH-LANG: Against the two bladed lance.

MONKEY: We fought for three hundred rounds –

ERH-LANG: Neither of us giving ground –

MONKEY: Until the three hundred and first round when I said the magic words 'Magic Monkey disappear'. And I disappeared –

ERH-LANG: And I did not know where the next blow would come from. So I made myself disappear too.

MONKEY: Then I reappeared, transformed into the shape of –

ERH-LANG: Erh-Lang. So I, not to be outdone, reappeared in the shape of –

MONKEY: Monkey. So each of us would have to kill ourselves to kill our enemy. Meanwhile the Jade Emperor…

SPIRIT OF THE PLANET VENUS: Found it most confusing.

JADE EMPEROR: Who do I cheer for, Spirit of the Planet Venus? Who do I cheer for?

MONKEY: Then I turned into a bee and stung Erh-Lang on the nose.

ERH-LANG: And so I turned into a flower to attract the bee to my nectar.

MONKEY: So I turned into an ox to eat the flower.

ERH-LANG: So I turned into tiger to eat the ox.

MONKEY: So I turned into a hunter's net to catch the tiger.

ERH-LANG: So I turned into a pair of scissors to cut the net.

MONKEY: So I turned into a stone to break the scissors.

ERH-LANG: So I turned into some paper.

*MONKEY and ERH-LANG are left playing 'Stone, Paper, Scissors'.*

And I said, 'I think we've just invented a game.'

MONKEY: And I said, 'I think I've just won it!'

*ERH-LANG keels over, exhausted.*

*The Eastern Heaven.*

SPIRIT OF THE PLANET VENUS: But then, through the air, tumbling round and round in a great light of enlightenment from the Western Heaven came…

ALL: Tathagata Father Buddha.

BUDDHA: And knowing all that is, was and shall be, I knew what had transpired here. Jade Emperor, I have heard this monkey's rumpus from my Western throne.

JADE EMPEROR: Please, Tathagata Father Buddha, if you know any way this monkey might be tamed please tell me. He has evaded Yama King of Death and eaten my peaches of eternal life and defeated my champion, Master of Illustrious Sagacity Erh-lang and quite ruined my afternoon green tea time.

BUDDHA: Force, I fear, will not subdue him. His nature is irrepressible. Nevertheless, this nature is flawed and no man or beast can help but be true to their nature. Therefore his own nature must be used to bring him to heel.

JADE EMPEROR: What do you mean, Tathagata Father Buddha?

BUDDHA: He can't resist playing games. So I shall play a game with him.

JADE EMPEROR: A game?

BUDDHA: You drink your tea and I shall see to Monkey.

*Flower-fruit Mountain.*

Are you Sun Wu-k'ung, the Handsome Monkey King?

MONKEY: That's me. Who are you?

BUDDHA: I am Tathagata Father Buddha.

MONKEY: The honour is all mine. What brings you to Flower-fruit Mountain?

BUDDHA: I have a game for us to play

MONKEY: Old Monkey does love to play.

BUDDHA: All you have to do is jump over my hand.

MONKEY: That's not much of a game. I am a magic monkey, I am master of the seventy-two transformations. I am master of the cloud trapeze, besides, I have a very big stick.

BUDDHA: Then you should find it an easy game to win.

MONKEY: And what do I win when I win?

BUDDHA: Everything you desire.

MONKEY: Sounds good to me.

BUDDHA: You haven't asked what you lose if you lose.

MONKEY: Monkey never loses. I shall jump to the ends of the world.

*MONKEY jumps.*

(*Off.*) You see. I have jumped to the end of the world.

BUDDHA: And what do you see?

MONKEY: (*Off.*) I see five pink pillars taller than the sky. I will  leave my signature here just so you don't try any monkey business.

*Sound of urination.*

BUDDHA: What are you doing now, you filthy monkey?

MONKEY: My signature. Monkeys cannot write.

BUDDHA: Come back at once you urinous beast.

*MONKEY returns.*

MONKEY: Now I would like everything I desire, if you don't mind, Tathagata Father Buddha.

BUDDHA: First smell my hand.

MONKEY: Smells remarkably like my signature.

BUDDHA: That is because you jumped no farther than my hand.

MONKEY: But I jumped to the end of the world.

BUDDHA: Buddha's whole world is but a grain of sand therefore a grain of sand is the whole world and the truly enlightened one holds that grain of sand in his hand.

MONKEY: What in creation are you talking about?

BUDDHA: If you've got to ask, you'll never know. Those five pink pillars you saw were my fingers.

MONKEY: What can you do to me? After all those peaches, I shall live forever.

*A mountain falls on MONKEY.*

BUDDHA: What is the point in living forever, if you do not do so wisely? You must learn that everything is nothing and nothingness is everything. Therefore you must experience what it is to have nothing. And that is not a lesson learnt in the blinking of a gnat's eye. No, no. You will need to learn patience too. Therefore, you shall be banished from the heavens to be locked up in Monkey Mountain for five hundred years. Above your head shall be the sacred inscription, 'Om Mane Padme Hum'.

MONKEY: You can't do this to Monkey. You cannot re-press Monkey like this. Monkey is irrepressible.

BUDDHA: The days of your punishment shall not end until a holy master comes needing your protection on a journey to fetch sacred scriptures from the Western Heaven. And in this way, perhaps you shall learn that to have nothing is to have everything, that to be most empty is to be most full.

*BUDDHA departs.*

MONKEY: What do you mean you crazy Buddha! You talk words but they make no sense. Ah! Ah! My nose is itchy. Let me out you crazy immortal!

YAMA: And when you do get out, you barbaric beast, I'll be waiting for you. Yama King of Death does not forget. I will return. Hahahah.

MONKEY: Let me out! Let me out my nose itches like anteater's nostril.

*Four hundred and ninety-nine years later.*

(*Exhausted.*) Please let me out… My nose… Four hundred and ninety-nine year itch… I can't take it anymore.

*The court of the EMPEROR OF CHINA.*

PRIME MINISTER: His most supreme and sublime excellency T'ai Tsang Emperor of China!

EMPEROR OF CHINA: O Great Tathagata Father Buddha, where has the world gone wrong? Bandits roam the countryside robbing, raping the innocent and pillaging the holy temples and pagodas which I have built in your honour. My people have forgotten your sacred laws which should govern human behaviour. Brother fights with brother, father fights with son, and mother fights with the woman next door while little sister sits in the corner crying. All act against their nature and your laws. O Great Tathagata Father Buddha, what can I do? When will peace reign in China?

*Thunder.*

PRIME MINISTER: We should go inside, Your Excellency, it looks like rain is going to reign in China.

EMPEROR OF CHINA: Quiet, Prime Minister, Buddha is answering, let me listen…(*Listening.*)…yes, I see…

PRIME MINISTER: What does he say Emperor T'ai Tsang?

EMPEROR OF CHINA: Be quiet Prime Minister, it is not a very good connection…(*Listening.*)…scriptures, I see, from where? …But that is very far…patience, I see…a holy master, I see… Hello? Hello? …the line is down.

PRIME MINISTER: What did he say?

EMPEROR OF CHINA: The Tathagata Father Buddha says I must find the holiest person in my Empire and they must make a pilgrimage of one hundred thousand leagues to the Western Heaven where Tathagata Father Buddha will give them sacred scriptures which govern the laws of heaven and of earth. And if we live by these laws, peace shall return to China. Hurry, Prime Minis-

21

ter, have your guards find me the holiest person in my realms. I won't be able to take much more of this.

PRIME MINISTER: Yes, Your Highness. So I sent the Imperial Guard to hunt high and low for the holiest person in all China, but so corrupt and lawless had the Empire become, this was no easy matter. Then, one evening, by the banks of the Yellow River they saw a young monk…

*Enter TRIPITAKA.*

TRIPITAKA: Your most high and wise Imperial Majesty of all China, T'ai Tsang.

EMPEROR OF CHINA: And your name is?

TRIPITAKA: Tripitaka, Your Highness.

EMPEROR OF CHINA: And you are the holiest person in my Empire?

TRIPITAKA: I am a humble monk, Your Highness, and make no claim for myself. I am what you see.

EMPEROR OF CHINA: Well, get up so I can see what you are. You think you are strong enough and brave enough to make this journey to the West to get these sacred scriptures? One hundred thousand leagues, through every sort of danger known to man.

TRIPITAKA: I am neither strong nor brave, but if it is Your Highness's desire that I should do so, I would die sooner and have my soul sent to hell rather than fail you.

EMPEROR OF CHINA: The body may be frail, but you have the heart of a warrior, Tripitaka. From now on I shall call you sister. You shall have the protection of a regiment from my Imperial guard. You shall have the finest stallion from the Imperial stables and a team of mules will carry two years worth of supplies from the Imperial stores.

TRIPITAKA: I require nothing but a begging bowl to beg for food, a passport to cross the many borders freely and three guards to protect me from the dangers of the way.

EMPEROR OF CHINA: Why make a difficult task more difficult?

TRIPITAKA: If I am to complete the task Buddha has set me, I must put my faith in Buddha not a hoard of guards. To be true to my nature which is the only way perfection might be attained, I must make this pilgrimage as is natural to all people, on foot and, as for food, I must trust to the generosity of the way.

EMPEROR OF CHINA: I see. Prime Minister, see that she has all that she requires. One last thing, Tripitaka?

TRIPITAKA: Yes, your highness?

EMPEROR OF CHINA: You will be gone a long time. How will I know when you are returning?

TRIPITAKA: When that tree that faces West turns back towards the East, I shall be coming home.

EMPEROR OF CHINA: Here.

TRIPITAKA: What is this?

EMPEROR OF CHINA: Some earth from your homeland so you might remember us.

*The journey commences.*

TRIPITAKA: O Father Buddha, few are the pilgrims that have walked this way. Beyond cities, beyond towns, beyond the furthest farms and up the jagged paths of Monkey Mountain where the cold streams and wildblast bushes make one sad and think of home. Forgive me Father Buddha but I am afraid.

BUDDHA: Though you might not be the bravest human

soul, you are the most perfect having practised your
holiness for ten incarnations. For that reason you must
be especially careful, for if the demons and the monsters
of the way taste but a morsel of your flesh, they will live
forever. Take this.

*A golden headband.*

TRIPITAKA: What is it for?

BUDDHA: So you can rely on your travelling companion's help.

TRIPITAKA: But of course I can rely on them, they are
the Emperor's own guards.

BUDDHA: Just say the magic prayer and all shall be well.

*BUDDHA laughs and disappears.*

TRIPITAKA: Buddha? Buddha, where have you gone?

*A different laugh. The laugh of GENERAL YIN.*

GENERAL YIN: Smell her, smell her and she's coming
this way. Perfection, perfection, I smell the perfect dinner.

TRIPITAKA: What was that?

GENERAL YIN: Seize them! Seize them!

A DEMON: Yes sir, General Yin!

*A horde of DEMONS descend upon them led by GEN-
ERAL YIN, a tiger monster.*

GENERAL YIN: The perfect dinner, my demon friends!

A DEMON: Yes sir, General Yin.

A DEMON: But this one's all skinny, General!

GENERAL YIN: Skinny perhaps but quite perfect.

A DEMON: But there's not much of her to go round.

GENERAL YIN: If we taste but a morsel of her flesh, we shall live forever. String her up. Let us feast upon the guards tonight to satisfy our bodily hunger and in the morning we shall have the monk as a continental breakfast. And then, then eternal life.

A DEMON: What's a continental breakfast, General Yin?

GENERAL YIN: It's a new concept I'm working on. It's like a meal only skinnier. I'm so glad we could have our friends from the Imperial Guard for dinner.

A DEMON: What's it to be, General Yin?

GENERAL YIN: Boiled egg and soldiers all round.

*They eat the three guards and promptly fall asleep.*

TRIPITAKA: This is shocking beyond belief. What am I to do? Barely have I set off to the West and my guards have been eaten and I shall be eaten in the morning. I shall go to hell for not fulfilling the Emperor's command. There's no hope for it. I must prepare to die.

MONKEY: Ah… Ah… AHH…

TRIPITAKA: What's that noise?

MONKEY: …Chooooooooooo! That's better.

TRIPITAKA: What's that? Who's there? Another demon?

MONKEY: What's that noise? Who said that?

TRIPITAKA: What's that? A monkey?

MONKEY: Who's that? A monk?

TRIPITAKA: What are you doing stuck in a mountain?

MONKEY: What are you doing all tied up on a mountain?

TRIPITAKA: A demon called General Yin has eaten my
guards and he plans to eat me for something called a
continental breakfast so that he can live forever. Can
you help me?

MONKEY: Why should I help you if you can't help me?

TRIPITAKA: But if you don't help me, I will never get to
the Western Heaven.

MONKEY: You're travelling to the Western Heaven? Why
didn't you say so before? I've been waiting for you. Five
hundred years, to be precise. You are a holy master
aren't you?

TRIPITAKA: I am a humble monk.

MONKEY: In that case, I'm sorry, I can't help. I have to
wait for a holy master.

TRIPITAKA: Now I'll never get the sacred scriptures from
the Buddha.

MONKEY: Did you say sacred scriptures? Then you must
be a master. You're far too humble. Come on, get me
out of here.

TRIPITAKA: But I have no chisel or axe.

MONKEY: All you have to do is say the magic words.
Above my head.

TRIPITAKA: I hope you're a good monkey.

MONKEY: I'm the best.

TRIPITAKA: (*Reading.*) Om Mane Padme Hum.

*Nothing.*

MONKEY: Call yourself a master.

TRIPITAKA: I didn't, you did.

MONKEY: Perhaps if we ask them.

26

TRIPITAKA: Who?

MONKEY: Them, the mountain spirits.

TRIPITAKA: I can't see them.

MONKEY: It takes a while to see them. About four hundred and ninety-nine years.

TRIPITAKA: (*With audience.*) Om Mane Padme Hum.

*The Mountain cracks open and MONKEY jumps free.*

MONKEY: Yippee, yippee, old Monkey's free! Come on.

*MONKEY calls a cloud.*

TRIPITAKA: What are you doing?

MONKEY: Taking you to the West. I am a master, amongst other things, of the Cloud Trapeze. We'll be there before you can say Peking Duck. And then old Monkey shall return to Flower-fruit Mountain and have another rumpus.

TRIPITAKA: But we can't fly.

MONKEY: You can't, but I can. I'll take you.

TRIPITAKA: No, we must go by foot.

MONKEY: You mean walk?

TRIPITAKA: To make a true pilgrimage, one must be true to one's nature. It is natural for a human to walk.

MONKEY: But it's ninety-nine thousand leagues at the very least.

TRIPITAKA: Well, if we want it to be shorter, we should get going.

*Growling.*

What's that?

MONKEY: Excuse me, bananas –

TRIPITAKA: The demons.

GENERAL YIN: Did I order my continental breakfast to go?

A DEMON: No sir, General Yin, you didn't.

GENERAL YIN: Then why is it going? Seize them my demon friends!

MONKEY: Leave this to me, master. It's time to play – !

*MONKEY fights and kills first the DEMONS and finally GENERAL YIN.*

You won't attack a holy master in a hurry again, my friend General Yin. See, Master, he wasn't a demon, Master. He was a monster, Master. He must have been sent to earth in this form as a punishment like me. In fact, his skin would make a very nice tiger-skin shirt for a handsome monkey that I know.

TRIPITAKA: Monkey!

MONKEY: Yes, Master?

TRIPITAKA: You killed them.

MONKEY: Well they killed your guards.

TRIPITAKA: You should only fight to defend yourself.

MONKEY: Attack is the best form of defence.

TRIPITAKA: Don't try and defend the indefensible.

MONKEY: Don't attack me for defending you.

TRIPITAKA: Don't confuse me, you infernal monkey! You must not kill monsters. They are here to atone for their sins just like you. How will they ever become enlightened if you go around killing them? I do not believe that you are a suitable companion for me on this journey.

MONKEY: Fine by me. See you later, alligator!

*MONKEY flies off.*

TRIPITAKA: Alone again! What am I to do?

*TRIPITAKA takes out the golden headband.*

What am I to do with this? Buddha said I could use it to rely on my companion's help, but now I have no companions. What did he mean? Which magic words? Perhaps he meant the magic words over Monkey's head. What were they again? Om Mane Padme Hum.

*MONKEY flies back.*

MONKEY: I was just passing on a cloud and I couldn't help but notice that pretty cool golden headband and I thought that is just the kind of accessory a Handsome Monkey King needs to go with a tiger-skin shirt. May I?

*No response.*

I'll take that as a yes, shall I?

*MONKEY puts on the headband.*

TRIPITAKA: Om Mane Padme Hum.

*MONKEY falls to the ground in agony.*

MONKEY: Stop, stop, please! The headband is squeezing my head. I can't get it off. You did this on purpose. Please stop or my head will be monkey brain soup.

TRIPITAKA: Om Mane Padme Hum.

MONKEY: It's not fair. It's not fair. You are a tricky master.

TRIPITAKA: A trickster monkey needs a tricky master, but a good monkey will find a grateful master. I see now that Buddha has ordained that you are to be my companion. We must go, we've wasted enough time already.

MONKEY: No, I'm not going, you cheated.

TRIPITAKA: You wanted the headband, it was your own nature that tricked you. Om Mane –

MONKEY: Okay, okay. I'm coming.

TRIPITAKA: And don't forget my bags.

MONKEY: (*Raises his stick.*) Ow my head! I'm coming, Master.

*They journey.*

Was five hundred years locked in a mountain not enough of a price to pay? You'd think at the very least I'd be able to enjoy a little fight or two. But no. What do I get? A headband that bursts my brains if I so much as think bad thoughts. And these bags... I'm tired, Master, are we nearly there?

*A farm.*

TRIPITAKA: Patience, Monkey, patience. We are not nearly there and we must find somewhere for the night. This boy might be able to help us. Boy?

BOY: What?

MONKEY: Don't say what, say pardon!

BOY: Who's your ugly friend?

MONKEY: She's not ugly, and I've got a big stick. Can I hit him with it, Master? Please?

TRIPITAKA: You cannot. Boy, is there a farmhouse near where we might beg a night's shelter?

BOY: There's Mr Kao's farm.

MONKEY: Mr Cow! And I suppose he's married to Mrs Pig.

BOY: K-A-O. Kao. The pig is his son in law.

MONKEY: And I suppose you're the dog's boll–

*TRIPITAKA makes to pray.*

MONKEY: Ow! Ow!

TRIPITAKA: What do you mean the pig's his son in law?

BOY: Three years ago Mr Kao's daughter was carried off to that toolshed by a pig monster where he now keeps her as a prisoner while he goes out foraging for food with his muck rake.

TRIPITAKA: And what did Mr Kao do about this?

BOY: He said, 'A pig in the family is no good thing, no good thing at all.'

MONKEY: Did he not try to persuade the pig monster to leave?

BOY: He did but the monster scraped his head something rotten with his muck rake, so that's why he's sent me to look for a holy monk who might exorcise the beast.

MONKEY: Well she's your monk and I'm your monkey. I'll give that pig monster some exercise with my magic stick.

TRIPITAKA: He means 'exorcise', to rid someone or something of a evil spirit.

MONKEY: I'm good at that too.

*MR KAO enters, sees MONKEY and then hides behind the boy, terrified.*

KAO: Is a pig monster not bad enough, but now I have a monkey monster too?

MONKEY: Is this Mr Kao or Mr Kao-ard? Hee-hee-hee.

*No response.*

Hey, let's not lose our senses of humour here.

KAO: Get off my farm! All of you monsters of nature leave me alone.

TRIPITAKA: I am a pilgrim monk from China and I am travelling to the Western Heaven to get scriptures from Tathagata Father Buddha. We were looking for shelter for the night.

KAO: Are you any good at fighting pig monsters?

MONKEY: A good fight would really cheer me up.

TRIPITAKA: My disciple means that he will be happy to rid you of this pig monster, without hurting anyone.

MONKEY: But why catch a monster if you can't hurt him?

TRIPITAKA: Om Mane –

MONKEY: Not my handsome monkey head again. Okay, okay. Where's this stupid pig?

KAO: Out foraging.

*A toolshed.*

MONKEY: And this is the toolshed where he has locked up your daughter?

KAO: Can't you hear her crying. My poor Number Three Daughter.

MONKEY: Well, where's the key then?

KAO: If I had the key, don't you think I'd have let her out before now?

MONKEY: Like I said, we don't want to lose our senses of humour as well as our daughters.

KAO: You better sort this pig out you cheeky monkey or I'll –

MONKEY: One, two, three.

*MONKEY blows; the door disappears.*

Call your daughter out then.

KAO: Oh my Number Three Daughter!

DAUGHTER: Daddy Kao!

KAO: You are safe now, Number Three!

DAUGHTER: But what will Pigsy do when he finds me gone, Daddy Kao?

MONKEY: But you will be there. Transform into Daughter Number Three!

*MONKEY transforms into DAUGHTER NUMBER THREE.*

I am master of the seventy-two transformations, I shall take your place and find out if he is a monster, Master, or just some ordinary demon. You take my master to your house and take good care of her.

*The others leave.*

Now, if I'm to convince this pig that I'm a real girl what should I do?

*PIGSY enters while MONKEY practices being a girl.*

PIGSY: And what are you doing out of your shed, pig-wife?

MONKEY: And what time of day do you call this?

PIGSY: Since when do you talk to me like that? Remember who's the pig around here.

MONKEY: Well, that's what I want to talk to you about. As you know my father, Daddy Kao, thinks that a pig in the family is, well, a bit of an embarrassment. Especially as we don't know the first thing about your family.

PIGSY: I didn't have a family. I was once a general in the

Jade Emperor's Water Army in the Eastern Heaven but I had too much wine at a party and tried to kiss the Goddess of the Moon. She was so furious that she had the Jade Emperor have me reborn onto the earth as a pig as punishment.

MONKEY: So, you're no ordinary Pig-monster?

PIGSY: No, I'm the piggest monster of them all. (*He cries.*) Give me a kiss my little porkpie.

MONKEY: Kiss you?

PIGSY: Are you forgetting my nine-pronged rake?

MONKEY: What is a girl to do? Should I kiss the smelly pig? Well, in for a fen, in for a yuan…

*MONKEY gives PIGSY a big kiss. PIGSY stands back.*

PIGSY: What strong lips you have, pig-wife!

MONKEY: All the better to kiss you with.

PIGSY: What long arms you have!

MONKEY: All the better to hold my stick.

PIGSY: What a big stick you have!

MONKEY: All the better to give your hide a crackling.

PIGSY: O my god, I kissed a monkey.

MONKEY: You think that's bad, I was that monkey. (*Worried.*) And I quite enjoyed it –

*They fight. Neither can overcome the other. MONKEY pins PIGSY's rake to the ground with his stick.*

I see that's no common or garden muck rake.

PIGSY: The Jade Emperor gave it to me as a reward for bravery in battle.

MONKEY: Did the Jade Emperor tell you how long your

punishment was to last?

PIGSY: I was told that I would be released from my punishment if I accompanied a monk on a journey to the West to get some scriptures from the Buddha.

MONKEY: That is a coincidence. I'm accompanying a monk on a journey to the West to get some scriptures from the Buddha.

*PIGSY and the MONKEYS stop fighting.*

PIGSY: Well why didn't you say so before?

MONKEY: Why didn't you ask?

*MONKEY knocks out PIGSY.*

And from now on, you can carry the bags.

*The journey continues. On the banks of the River of Flowing Sands. Blizzard. A Chinese Fish DRAGON shimmers through stage and auditorium then out. Enter TRIPITAKA, MONKEY and PIGSY.*

PIGSY: Was three years as a pig not enough of a price to pay? You'd think at the very least I'd be able to run around and play a little. But no! What do I get? Wind and snow and these bags. That tricky monkey! I'm tired, I'm hungry, are we nearly there?

MONKEY: No, we are not nearly there you lazy Pig. You must learn patience. Are we nearly there, Master?

TRIPITAKA: No, we are not nearly there, and this is a bitter storm, and here is a river too wide for us to cross. Sometimes I fear we shall never get there.

PIGSY: (*Reading a sign.*) 'The River of the Flowing Sands.'

MONKEY: We have come all this way, Master, do not lose heart. I'll come with you and find some shelter. Pigsy, you stay here and watch the bags.

*MONKEY and TRIPITAKA go. PIGSY is left on his*

35

*own.*

PIGSY: Do that, carry this, mind those. What do they think I am? Some kind of animal?

*DRAGON enters. PIGSY does not see it. It goes to eat PIGSY who unwittingly walks away.*

I don't like it. I smell a rat. Or something. Something fishy. (*To audience.*) Do you smell something fishy? You would tell me if you saw something, wouldn't you?

*DRAGON enters and tries to eat him.*

What? I can't hear you with all the wind. A what?

*He looks. There's nothing there.*

What are you talking about? I'll just put down my load for a minute and take a look.

*DRAGON enters once more unseen by PIGSY.*

No, can't see anything.

*PIGSY sits and eats a turnip. DRAGON eats his bags. DRAGON exits. PIGSY finishes turnip. Gets up.*

Where are the bags? Which one of you took my bags? Tell me or I'll take my muck rake to you. It was you. You look like just the sort who'd take a poor pig's bags.

*He is about to attack a member of the audience with his rake when the DRAGON enters. PIGSY runs off hysterically into the arms of MONKEY. DRAGON disappears.*

MONKEY: What are you doing, you lazy swine? Where are the bags? We need to pitch a tent until the storm is over.

PIGSY: The bags... Fish Dragon... Very big... Ate them.

MONKEY: What are you talking about? You ate them,

you greedy pig. Fish Dragon indeed. There are no Fish Dragons around here.

*DRAGON is behind MONKEY.*

Apart from that Fish Dragon, of course.

*They both panic. Fight with DRAGON.*

MONKEY: Magic stick, it's time –

*Fight between DRAGON, MONKEY and PIGSY. The DRAGON does not seem to tire.*

This Fish Dragon is fishier than I first thought. You keep him busy, Pigsy, I'll go consult with Tathagata Father Buddha. Back in a mo.

PIGSY: Brother Monkey…don't leave me, Brother Monkey!

*MONKEY cloud trapezes to confer with BUDDHA. PIGSY with many squeals and hollerings continues to fight the DRAGON.*

BUDDHA: What are you doing here, Monkey? You should be looking after Tripitaka.

MONKEY: (*Interrupted by PIGSY's shouts.*) There was a storm…and we came to a river…and Pigsy…will you excuse me one minute Tathagata Father Buddha?

PIGSY: Help me, help me Monkey, he's got me. This is it, the end of the line, Mr Pig is on the chopping block, the watery grave, the final curtain, good bye cruel world –

MONKEY: (*Shouting down to PIGSY.*) Will you keep it down, you stupid pig, I am trying to talk to Tathagata Father Buddha.

*PIGSY continues in dumb-show.*

That's better. Where was I, Tathagata Father Buddha? Yes, you see there was this Fish Dragon and we tried all our fighting tricks but does not seem to be tiring.

BUDDHA: You silly Monkey, you are always too quick to start a fight and too slow to start a conversation. Why did you not tell the Dragon that you were escorting a monk from China to the Western Heaven?

MONKEY: He didn't seem in the mood for a chat, Tathagata Father Buddha.

BUDDHA: He too is a monster who has fallen from heaven's grace and must make the journey with you to the West as penance. Go to him and shout Sandy and he will reveal his true shape.

MONKEY: Why didn't you say so before. Sandy!

*THE DRAGON stops and PIGSY seizes the moment and cuts his head off.*

BUDDHA: I did say go to him and say it.

*MONKEY returns to PIGSY.*

PIGSY: Look Monkey, I killed him. All on my own. I'm the best fighter. I'm the best –

MONKEY: You stupid pig. He was another disciple for our master. He was meant to come with us. How often have I told you; you should only fight to defend yourself.

PIGSY: But attack is the best form of defence.

MONKEY: Defend this, porkchop!

*MONKEY flattens him.*

Now, what are we going to do? And what is that smell? Is that you, you filthy pig?

PIGSY: I thought it was you, but I was too polite to say.

MONKEY: It's coming from the fish dragon. Listen, I hear a moaning.

PIGSY: There's someone in here and he's still alive. What

should we do, Monkey?

MONKEY: Where were you pigs when the Buddha of creation was handing out the brain cells. Pull him out, you crinkle cut pork-scratching.

*They do so.*

PIGSY: Is everyone we meet going to become a disciple?

MONKEY: When the master set off she had three guards who were eaten, now she has the three of us to guard her on the journey to the West.

PIGSY: How do we know this Sandy character isn't just some plain old demon pretending to be a monster so that he can eat us?

SANDY: A demon! I am a monster, I'll have you know. I was the chariot driver of the Jade Emperor but, because I am a clumsy oaf and broke a crystal ball at a peach festival, I was turned into a Fish Dragon and banished to this River of the Flowing Sands where the wild wind always stormed. Because of the hunger and the cold I used to come ashore to eat the odd traveller. That is why I wear these skulls about my neck to remind myself how low I've fallen. I am the most wretched of creatures.

PIGSY: And one of the smelliest.

SANDY: Yes. Even I can't bear my own smell.

PIGSY: No, but you can bear the bags.

SANDY: I had a feeling you were going to say that.

MONKEY: Enough, the blizzard is over, and we have to get across this river.

SANDY: We could use my old fish dragon skin.

MONKEY: Perhaps I won't have to do all the thinking round here from now on. Welcome aboard, Sandy. I'll get the master.

PIGSY: He might be able to think, but he's still going to carry the bags.

*They sail across the river. They reach the other side. The stage is bare.*

SANDY: Was five years as a Fish Dragon not enough of a price to pay? You'd think I'd be able to relax and write some pessimistic poetry. But no! What do I get? These bags and that puffed-up pig! Pigsy, are we nearly there?

PIGSY: Monkey, are we nearly – ?

MONKEY: Master, are we – ?

TRIPITAKA: No, my friends, we are not nearly there.

MONKEY: Sandy?

SANDY: Monkey?

MONKEY: Did any of the travellers you ate happen to mention before you ate them what land lay on the far side of the River of the Flowing Sands?

SANDY: One rather chewy chopstick salesman did tell me. This is the Forest of the Sky, it leads to the Cliffs of Despair.

PIGSY: This? A forest? Pull my other trotter.

*A forest of Chinese lanterns falls from the sky. The last one lands on PIGSY.*

Why does it always happen to me?

*Enter LITTLE OLD LADY and TWO LITTLE BOYS.*

LITTLE OLD LADY: Spare a penny for an old lady and her two sickly sons.

TRIPITAKA: I'm sorry, but we ourselves are poor monks

–

*MONKEY beats them into the ground.*

TRIPITAKA: Monkey! How often have I told you not to hit people unless you are provoked!

MONKEY: I'm sorry, Master, but they were demons, Master.

TRIPITAKA: It wasn't a demon, it was an old lady and her two sickly sons. You do that again and I'm afraid I will have to use the…

*TRIPITAKA makes the headband gesture.*

MONKEY: No, Master, please.

TRIPITAKA: Then no more unprovoked violence.

*They walk on. AN OLD MAN and his TWO DAUGH-TERS.*

LITTLE OLD MAN: Spare a penny for a little old man and his two deaf daughters.

TRIPITAKA: I'm sorry, but we ourselves are poor monks

–

*MONKEY beats them into the ground.*

Monkey! You've done it again.

MONKEY: But it was a demon, Master, I swear. I just can't control my stick when I smell a demon.

TRIPITAKA: It wasn't a demon, it was a little old man and his two deaf daughters. I warned you before. Om Mane Padme Hum.

MONKEY: You shall burst my brains.

TRIPITAKA: If this happens again, Monkey, I'm afraid you won't be able to come any further with us.

*They walk off. Enter THE LITTLE OLD MAN and his TWO DAUGHTERS, they reveal themselves to be MOTHER DEMON, WILY WORM and SLY DEVIL.*

MOTHER DEMON: Ha, it's working! Soon that Priest will send that Magic Monkey away and he'll be as defenceless as a turtle without his shell. We'll be munching on monk and wonton soup tonight and then…and then I shall live forever. Hahahahah. Have you set a fire beneath the wok, Wily Worm?

WILY WORM: Yes, Mother Demon.

MOTHER DEMON: Have you chopped the vegetables, Sly Devil.

SLY DEVIL: They are a pile of crudities, Mother Demon.

WILY WORM: What about the pig and the smelly sand monster, Mother Demon?

MOTHER DEMON: We shall soak them in water, peel back their skins, pickle them with salt, sun dry them and they'll be fine appetizers with a glass of wine on a cloudy day. Or perhaps we'll just chuck them into the soup. Now what shall we dress ourselves as to get rid of this pesky Monkey once and for all?

SLY DEVIL: What about a monk and his disciples?

MOTHER DEMON: Sly Devil by name, sly devil by nature! Transform!

*They transform themselves, TRIPITAKA and disciples enter, they meet the disguised demons.*

PRIEST: Spare a penny for an old priest and his two disappointing disciples.

TRIPITAKA: I'm sorry, but we ourselves – Monkey no!

*MONKEY has flattened them again.*

Monkey, I warned you!

MONKEY: But they were, they really were demons, really.

TRIPITAKA: They were a priest and his disappointing
disciples just like us. And I am disappointed in you.
I warned you if you used violence again without being provoked you could no longer remain a disciple of
mine.

MONKEY: But Master –

TRIPITAKA: No buts about it. What kind of a holy master
would I be if I let my disciples go round the country
killing aged citizens. You must leave me.

MONKEY: But – ?

TRIPITAKA: No.

PIGSY: Haha, brother Monkey. I might be stupid, but at
least I'm on the road to enlightenment. Whatever that
is.

*MONKEY leaves. Grisly sound.*

SANDY: What was that?

PIGSY: I'm scared. Monkey, come back!

SANDY: Demons, quick, run.

MOTHER DEMON: Run them to the Cliffs of Despair,
my devilish friends. Bring the wok of boiling water,
Wily Worm.

*Exit MONKEY for Flower-fruit Mountain while the
chase begins. TRIPITAKA, PIGSY and SANDY are
left hanging from the cliffs.*

*The Cliffs of Despair.*

SLY DEVIL: We have them, Mother Demon.

WILY WORM: Mother Demon, the wok is underneath

them.

MOTHER DEMON: Excellent, excellent work my young devils.

SANDY: I've got a bad feeling about this.

PIGSY: Master?

TRIPITAKA: Yes, Pigsy?

PIGSY: Isn't that a giant wok of boiling water underneath us?

TRIPITAKA: Yes, Pigsy.

PIGSY: Master?

TRIPITAKA: What is it, Pigsy?

PIGSY: Why do you think this is called the Cliff of Despair.

TRIPITAKA: Use your brain Pigsy.

*Pause. PIGSY uses his brain.*

PIGSY: I think I understand it now.

*Pause.*

TRIPITAKA/PIGSY/SANDY: Help! Help! Help us, Monkey!

*End of Act One.*

# ACT TWO

BUDDHA: Where were we?

*TRIPITAKA, PIGSY and SANDY are now falling from the Cliffs of Despair into a giant wok.*

TRIPITAKA/PIGSY/SANDY: Help! Help! Help us, Monkey!

BUDDHA: Ah yes, that's it, falling from the Cliffs of Despair. It seemed a hopeless situation.

*BUDDHA chuckles.*

TRIPITAKA: The situation seems hopeless, my friends. We shall all go to hell for failing to fulfil the Emperor's command.

SANDY: Excuse me, Master.

*They stop falling.*

TRIPITAKA: What is it, Sandy?

SANDY: Well, though I do not have the magic powers of Monkey, nor the brute strength of Pigsy, I do have one special ability which might be of some use at this particular point in time.

TRIPITAKA: What's that, Sandy?

SANDY: The ability to be in two places at the one time.

TRIPITAKA: That might help you, but how will it help Pigsy and I?

SANDY: I could go to Flower-fruit Mountain to persuade Monkey to come back.

TRIPITAKA: Perhaps it might work.

*They recommence falling. Meanwhile on Flower-fruit Mountain…*

SANDY: …walking by the Cliffs of Despair.

MONKEY: Walking you say?

SANDY: Yes. And a great wind…

MONKEY: A great wind you say?

SANDY: Yes.

MONKEY: I myself recently had cause to make a great wind.

SANDY: Bannanas?

MONKEY: Yes!

SANDY: Yes and we are currently falling into a wok of boiling water.

*The Cliffs of Despair. TRIPITAKA, PIGSY and SANDY are still falling.*

MOTHER DEMON: Is it boiling Wily Worm?

WILY WORM: Yes, Mother Demon.

MOTHER DEMON: And the wontons, Sly Devil?

SLY DEVIL: The wontons have been warmed, Mother Demon.

MOTHER DEMON: Yum-yum, Pig's bum.

PIGSY: Get your lousy stinking hands off my bum. This pig is not for eating.

*Flower-fruit Mountain.*

MONKEY: Monk and Wonton Soup, you say?

SANDY: Yes. Please save us, Monkey.

MONKEY: But Tripitaka has banished me.

SANDY: She forgives you now.

MONKEY: She does?

SANDY: She does.

MONKEY: How much?

SANDY: Forgives you for everything.

MONKEY: Well, it looks as if it's that time again.

*MONKEY returns to the Cliffs of Despair. He fights DEMON MOTHER, WILY WORM and SLY DEVIL while juggling his three friends above the wok of boiling water. TRIPITAKA, being so light, is shot through the rafters by him. MONKEY defeats the THREE DEMONS by knocking them into the wok. MONKEY, PIGSY and SANDY reunite.*

PIGSY: Where's Tripitaka?

*They all look up. TRIPITAKA comes hurtling back from the rafters, lands on PIGSY's shoulders, flattens him. He picks himself up and dusts himself down.*

TRIPITAKA: Thank you for breaking my fall, Pigsy.

PIGSY: Why me?

MONKEY: Forgive me, Master, for the acts of unprovoked violence.

TRIPITAKA: No, forgive me, Monkey, I was wrong, they were demons. I... I am sorry.

MONKEY: (*Embarrassed, blushing.*) It was...it was nothing, master.

*Pause.*

SANDY: Ahem, shouldn't we be moving on?

*Night-time. A GHOST. All except TRIPITAKA sleep.*

GHOST: Master!

47

TRIPITAKA: What? Who's there? Not more demons?

GHOST: I am not a demon. Look closely and you will see what I am.

*GHOST reveals himself as a king.*

TRIPITAKA: I beg your pardon, Your Majesty. Of what city are you king?

GHOST: The city of Black Rooster.

TRIPITAKA: Were you a bad king? Did your people throw you out?

GHOST: No, I was a good king, but six years ago in my city there was a drought. Not a grain of rice grew in the fields. All my people were dying of hunger.

TRIPITAKA: Heaven favours where virtue rules. You should have opened your storehouses and helped your people.

GHOST: My own storehouses were empty too. I suffered with my people. For three years this went on. We were on the brink of starvation when a magician came along and, with a wave of his wand, the rivers flowed again, the wells filled and the heavens opened. The magician became my closest friend. But, one day as we were walking in the flower garden, we came to a well and with a great shove, the magician pushed me in. He covered the well with a paving stone and planted a banana tree on top of it. I have been dead for three years while the magician turned himself into the image of me and now rules in my place.

TRIPITAKA: You mean you're…you're a ghost?

GHOST: Please, do not be afraid. I've come to you only to ask your help. The Dragon King of the well that my body lies in told me that you are a great master and that your disciple Monkey is very good at dealing with fiends and monsters.

TRIPITAKA: But how do I know that you are not a fiend or a monster and that the king who rules in Black Rooster is the true king?

GHOST: The fiend who rules there now brings up my son as if he was his own, but he refuses to let him see his mother, the queen, since they might discuss how I have changed. Besides, when the magician pushed me into the well, I had this jade tablet which is the seal of my kingship. I give it to you so that you might persuade the queen and my son that I am the true king.

*GHOST gives TRIPITAKA a jade tablet.*

TRIPITAKA: Monkey! Monkey wake up. Someone needs our help.

MONKEY: Why can't people learn to help themselves. I always help myself.

TRIPITAKA: Yes, but by helping yourself, you have helped so many beings return to their own good nature and rid the world of so many demons.

MONKEY: But I'm tired.

TRIPITAKA: Remember, Monkey, to save one life is better than building a seven storey pagoda.

MONKEY: This is true. So Tripitaka told me the story and I hatched a cunning monkey plan so we might find out who the real king really was. At first light I turned Pigsy and Sandy into hares –

PIGSY: Pigs have bristles, not hairs.

MONKEY: A hare. A big rabbit. Transform!

SANDY: (*Laughing.*) A pig rabbit, you mean.

*SANDY is changed into a hare too.*

PIGSY: Look who's talking, fish face.

TRIPITAKA: And the prince of Black Rooster who was out hunting chased the hares and they led him to Monkey and Tripitaka –

*Enter PIGSY and SANDY with arrows sticking out of their bottoms.*

PIGSY/SANDY: Ow! Ow! Ow!

*PRINCE enters on horseback.*

PRINCE: Hey, you monk, what have you done with those hares I was chasing?

TRIPITAKA: So Monkey and I told the young prince the story the ghost had told us and he did not believe so we showed him the jade tablet, and still the prince could not bring himself to believe that his father had been dead three years and that a magician had taken his place so the Prince went to ask his mother.

PRINCE: Mother there is something I must ask you.

QUEEN: Anything, a son should be able to ask his mother anything.

PRINCE: Is my father different to how he was three years ago. And the queen, my mother, stopped and then sadly said –

QUEEN: O my son, what was three years ago warm and full of sunshine, is now cold as ice. He's not the man I married. But why ask me that now?

PRINCE: And so I told her of the travellers I had met and their strange story and how they had told me not to say a word to the magician king until they themselves arrived at court, but to carry on as normal.

MONKEY: Meanwhile me and Pigsy –

SANDY: No, it's Pigsy and I.

MONKEY: No, Sandy, you're looking after Tripitaka. Me and Pigsy went to the well into which the magician had pushed the real king. I sent Pigsy down to fetch the body.

PIGSY: (*From the bottom of a well.*) Why is it always me who has to do the hard work?

MONKEY: Because it's me who does all the hard thinking. And when Pigsy came up from the well with the body, Buddha returned the real king to life. We all then proceeded to the court with the real king disguised so that the false king might not suspect anything.

*Enter FALSE KING OF BLACK ROOSTER and the QUEEN.*

FALSE KING: What were you doing talking to him. I expressly ordered you not to talk to the prince.

QUEEN: He is my son. I have a right –

FALSE KING: You have no rights here, I am the king.

*Enter PRINCE.*

PRINCE: Father, some monks have arrived at the court begging food and shelter.

FALSE KING: Begging monks? Send them in and I will teach them to beg from me.

*Enter the four MONKS and the disguised TRUE KING OF BLACK ROOSTER.*

Who are you?

TRIPITAKA: I am Tripitaka, I am travelling to the Western Heaven to fetch scriptures for the Emperor of China.

FALSE KING: And who are your disciples? Passports, come on, I don't have all day.

TRIPITAKA: Passports, Monkey.

PIGSY: Pigsy.

SANDY: And Sandy.

FALSE KING: There are five of you. Who is the fifth?

TRIPITAKA: I might just as well ask you who you are.

FALSE KING: Don't be impertinent. I am the king, that's who I am.

TRIPITAKA: Are you? Are you really?

*MONKEY reveals the TRUE KING who is identical to the FALSE KING.*

MONKEY: And who's this? The monkey's uncle?

PIGSY: Is he really your uncle, Monkey? There's no resemblance.

MONKEY: Shut up, you stupid Pig!

*FALSE KING roars then flies up into the air.*

It's time to play.

*MONKEY flies up after him. They fight in the sky, then THE FALSE KING disappears. MONKEY is left fighting on his own. A second TRIPITAKA appears beside the real TRIPITAKA.*

I had him. I had him now where's that magician gone?

PIGSY: Monkey, he's here.

MONKEY: Where? I can't see him.

SANDY: He's turned himself into Tripitaka.

MONKEY: He can turn himself into what he likes but I'll get him.

*MONKEY brings his stick down on TRIPITAKA's head. TRIPITAKA uses her begging bowl to protect herself.*

TRIPITAKA: I knew that bowl would come in handy.

*MONKEY brings it down on the other TRIPITAKA's head. She also produces a bowl.*

SANDY: Please Monkey, you'll hurt the real Tripitaka.

PIGSY: But how do we tell which one is which?

MONKEY: I have a good idea. Which one of you is the real Tripitaka?

BOTH: I am.

MONKEY: Now I know one of you is not telling the truth, who's lying?

BOTH: She is.

MONKEY: So, you want to play hard to get do you? Then Monkey must put his thinking cap on.

PIGSY: That's it.

MONKEY: What is?

SANDY: The headband.

MONKEY: What about my headband?

PIGSY: Only the real Tripitaka knows how to make it hurt your head.

MONKEY: No, I have a formula, if only I can remember it. I have it, if one of them always lies, and one of them always tells the truth, how do you tell which one is which?

PIGSY/SANDY: We give up.

MONKEY: You ask them who the other one would say is the false Tripitaka. And she will say:

BOTH: She is the false Tripitaka.

*They both point at the real TRIPITAKA.*

MONKEY: Haha! That means it is the other who is the false Tripitaka. Seize her.

ALL: Huh?

MONKEY: Why do I have to work with amateurs! Look, real Tripitaka would say false Tripitaka would say that real Tripitaka is the false Tripitaka. False Tripitaka would think that real Tripitaka would say that false Tripitaka is false Tripitaka but she always lies so she would change what she would say and say real Tripitaka is false Tripitaka. So therefore they both say that real Tripitaka is false Tripitaka and that's how we know the other is really the false Tripitaka.

PIGSY: Now you're making my head hurt you crazy monkey. Master, if you really are the master make his head hurt too.

TRIPITAKA: Om Mane Padme Hum.

MONKEY: Ow, you sneaky bacon, my brain feels like a pea with an elephant sitting on it.

PIGSY: Strange Monkey, your formula was right after all. Next time I am confronted by an inveterate liar and an honest man and a difficult decision I must remember it.

SANDY: In the meantime, my porcine friend, let's get this magician.

*Fight of many transformations and confusions. Begging bowl is used repeatedly to defend the various pilgrims.*

TRIPITAKA: This magician has too many tricks. We shall never get the sacred scriptures from the Western Heaven.

FALSE KING: Sacred scriptures? Why didn't you say so before?

SANDY: And so the False King told us that he was in fact the Blessed Blue Lion of Tathagata Father Buddha.

PIGSY: You mean heaven is to blame for all of this?

SANDY: And the False King replied:

FALSE KING: Heaven is to blame for nothing. Nature is as nature does.

SANDY: And Monkey said:

MONKEY: More crazy Buddha sayings.

TRIPITAKA: Please explain, Blessed Blue Lion of Tathagata Father Buddha.

SANDY: So the Blessed Blue Lion explained that:

PIGSY: The King of Black Rooster was a good king.

SANDY: So good that Buddha came here in the form of a priest to invite him to the Western Heaven.

PIGSY: But when the Tathagata Father Buddha came the king was rude to him and kept him waiting outside, starving and cold, for three days.

SANDY: So, in return, Tathagata Father Buddha sent three years of famine and then sent his lion in the form of a magician to throw his body down a well where it lay cold and starving, for another three years.

TRIPITAKA: Only to be released when a monk from China came seeking scriptures from the Western Heaven.

PIGSY: So by the efforts of Pigsy –

SANDY: And Sandy –

MONKEY: Not to mention Monkey –

SANDY: All was returned to its proper order. And then, in a puff of blue blessed smoke –

FALSE KING: The Blessed Blue Lion disappeared.

*The FALSE KING disappears in a puff of blue smoke. Pause.*

MONKEY: Sandy? Pigsy?

SANDY/PIGSY: Yes, Monkey?

MONKEY: If you've quite finished…

TRIPITAKA: It is now time for you, Your Majesty, to return to your throne and for us to return to our journey.

TRUE KING: No, I do not deserve the throne. Because of my rudeness to the Bodhisattva Manjusri, I have brought unhappiness to my family and my kingdom. One of you pilgrims would be a better king than I.

TRIPITAKA: I am but a humble monk, Your Majesty, and I have my own work to do.

TRUE KING: What about you, Monkey?

MONKEY: Once I was a king and all I desired was to be king of all I saw and play and fight forever. But now I see that to be king is to have so many cares – if the crops do not grow, if disease plagues the kingdom, if the other kings invade, the king must share the sadness of all his people. I have become used to this journeying life and must help Tripitaka on her way.

TRUE KING: Well said, Monkey, so I suppose I must return to my throne –

PIGSY: I'd like to be king.

MONKEY: (*Pulling him by the ear.*) We all must help Tripitaka on her way.

TRUE KING: Well, I will only return to my throne if you all join me in a vegetarian feast.

PIGSY: A feast? A feast is a kingdom to me. Even a vegetarian one.

MONKEY: And when we had feasted we set off once more.

*The pilgims travel on through various terrains and weathers. They grow more exhausted.*

YAMA: I'll be waiting for you, Monkey. You have cheated me long enough. Yama King of Death does not forget. I will see you at The River that Leads to Heaven. Hahahah.

SANDY: What was that?

MONKEY: (*Grimly.*) It was nothing. Let's keep going.

*They reach the bank of a river but are taken by the sight of something in the distance.*

SANDY: Look there…

PIGSY: In the distance…

MONKEY: Vulture Peak…

TRIPITAKA: And there, above the clouds, a temple…

MONKEY: Thunderclap Temple, home of Tathagata, the Buddha of the Western Heaven.

PIGSY: You mean we're nearly there?

TRIPITAKA: Look how it shines like a golden crown in the morning sky.

SANDY: Like the apex of the heavens.

PIGSY: Like…like a big, big thing up in the air. Let's go.

*PIGSY falls in the river.*

Who put this river here?

MONKEY: The River that Leads to Heaven. It is eight hundred leagues across.

SANDY: And of course, we've no boat –

TRIPITAKA: So near and yet so far. O my friends, when I left the Emperor of China I thought it would be easy to get to the Western Heaven. A couple of years at the most. And now we have been walking thirteen years and had to fight off every monster and demon and cross every high mountain and fathomless river in creation, and still we are not there. There is no hope.

MONKEY: Patience, master, patience, have faith in Father Buddha, a way shall be found. Meanwhile, let us rest here.

*They gradually fall asleep by the banks of the river. As they do so the river gradually turns to ice. YAMA KING OF DEATH laughs. This wakes PIGSY.*

PIGSY: What was that?

MONKEY: It was nothing, Pigsy, go back to sleep.

PIGSY: But look, Monkey, the river has turned to ice.

MONKEY: So it has.

PIGSY: Look, it's strong enough to stand on.

MONKEY: Master, Master!

PIGSY: Buddha be praised, he found a way.

SANDY: I have a very bad feeling about this. Perhaps we should wait a few days.

PIGSY: And wait for a boat to drop out of the sky?

TRIPITAKA: No, we have been on the road so long the Emperor of China will give up all hope if we delay much more.

MONKEY: Well then, let's put our skates on before it melts.

*Skating. A hole opens up in the ice. YAMA pops his head through then disappears. All but TRIPITAKA see the hole. They try to warn her but she skates straight into it.*

SANDY: Master!

PIGSY: Master!

MONKEY: Tripitaka!

SANDY: This is bad, this time it is really worse than bad.

PIGSY: What shall we do, Monkey?

MONKEY: I must rescue her.

SANDY: But she's under water and Tripitaka has no magic. She'll be drowned, if she's not already eaten. This is the end, I know it is.

MONKEY: Shut up, Sandy. I said I will go down and rescue her.

PIGSY: But you're a monkey, you hate water. It's enough your magic can do to stay alive under water. You won't be able to fight this monster.

MONKEY: Me and this monster go back a long way. It's me he wants, not Tripitaka. You two wait here. Transform into a monkeyfish!

*Underwater. TRIPITAKA lies dead upon a slab. MONKEY enters, swimming.*

Master? Master where are you? There you are Master, you must wake up and return to the surface. Master? Wake up? This is no ordinary monster, this is Yama King of Death. Please wake up, Master, it's me he wants, not you.

*MONKEY kisses her.*

Cold. She's dead!

YAMA: Ah my old friend, we meet again, still up to your old monkey business? I felt sure that we would meet again.

MONKEY: Yama, I've come to beg you to return my master Tripitaka to life.

YAMA: You? Coming to beg me? Well, that is a change.

Usually you choose to threaten me or beat me or van-
dalise my ledgers of death.

MONKEY: I have changed. I beg you.

YAMA: No.

MONKEY: What must I give you for you to change your
mind?

YAMA: What are you prepared to give me?

MONKEY: I have paid my punishment for the trouble I
caused in heaven and now I only wish to serve my master and attain true enlightenment. I would give anything
for her.

YAMA: And so you shall. So you shall. In return for her
life, I will take your life and then your soul, you dam-
nable monkey, and then I will have you reborn as the
lowest form of life – an amoeba or a blade of grass – so
it will take you all eternity to crawl back up to heaven.

MONKEY: If you want my life for hers you may have it.
However, I would ask you just one favour.

YAMA: What right have you to ask any favour of me?

MONKEY: I have no right but will ask it all the same.
That I might fulfil my promise to accompany Tripitaka
to the Western Heaven before you take my life so she at
least might attain enlightenment and eternal life.

YAMA: Since it is not something for yourself that you ask
I will allow it. And then, and then I shall have your life.
Look, a new book and it has your number on it: 1350.
This time you shall stick to it. And one thing more, you
shall not tell anyone of our little bargain or else I shall
take both your life and Tripitaka's.

*The River Bank. TRIPITAKA stands with SANDY and
PIGSY. MONKEY emerges slowly from the water.*

SANDY: Look, Monkey, look.

PIGSY: You did it.

SANDY: Our master is alive again.

TRIPITAKA: Monkey? Are you alright, Monkey?

MONKEY: Yes, Master, yes, I am alright. I am glad to see that we did not let you down when you needed us.

TRIPITAKA: Thank you, Monkey, I will not forget it.

MONKEY: But we still need to cross this River that Leads to Heaven.

PIGSY: That has been taken care of too. Look, there's a bridge that seems to lead to Buddha's Temple on Vulture Peak.

SANDY: But we don't know that. We can't see where it leads. It disappears into the clouds. What's holding it up?

TRIPITAKA: Faith. It is the Cloud Bridge of Faith. Faith holds it up.

SANDY: But how do we know we can trust our faith? It looks so long. We can't even see the end.

TRIPITAKA: Its length differs from one pilgrim to the next.

SANDY: How can that be?

TRIPITAKA: It depends on how many difficulties one has had in getting here.

PIGSY: But we have had endless difficulties.

SANDY: Then it will be an endless walk to the Western Heaven.

MONKEY: We have had eighty difficulties in getting here, so the bridge shall be eighty leagues long.

TRIPITAKA: What has happened to you dear Monkey?

61

MONKEY: Nothing, Master.

TRIPITAKA: Well, what is eighty leagues after what we have been through? Come on my friends, let us climb.

SANDY: It's going to collapse or there'll be a wind or something. We're going to fall, I know we are. We're going to fall and die!

TRIPITAKA: Have faith, Sandy. We must think of something to help you not be frightened. We will count away the miles and our disasters and your fears. Don't look back or down, look forward and count yourself to heaven.

*They count to eighty as they cross the bridge. At times it might seem that they will fall but they push on. Crescendo as they near heaven.*

SANDY: That's funny, we didn't fall.

PIGSY: Funny? I feel funny.

SANDY: You look funny too.

PIGSY: So do you, fish face.

SANDY: We're all golden.

TRIPITAKA: Because we are truly enlightened. We have left our earthly bodies behind. These are our heavenly bodies. We've done it. Thunderclap Temple.

*The gates of the temple open, BUDDHA is revealed.*

BUDDHA: Monk from the East, you are welcome to the Western Heaven.

*All prostrate themselves.*

TRIPITAKA: Tathagata Father Buddha, we have been sent by the Emperor of China to obtain sacred scriptures from you so that he might return his country to peace and harmony. Father Buddha, grant us this favour, we have travelled long and I fear that the Emperor will have given up on us long ago.

BUDDHA: I have here three baskets of scriptures that can save all people from the torments and afflictions of life. Together they describe the path to perfection. Since you have travelled far, I shall give them to you. Though I fear that the people of the earth will learn little from them since humans are generally foolish and boisterous except when they are young.

TRIPITAKA: Thank you Father Buddha, we are truly grateful.

BUDDHA: There are 5048 scrolls here, and you have been on the road for 5040 days. It would be most perfect if you were to return to China in eight days so there be one scroll for every day you have been away. You shall therefore return through the sky, carried on my own private magic carpet and in eight days you will be home in China.

TRIPITAKA: Thank you Father Buddha. We should get going.

BUDDHA: You should.

TRIPITAKA: Pigsy, Sandy, Monkey, come on.

MONKEY: I can't.

TRIPITAKA: Why not?

MONKEY: I can't say.

TRIPITAKA: Father Buddha, Monkey has not been himself since he saved me from the River that Leads to Heaven, perhaps you can help him find himself again.

BUDDHA: Monkey made a bargain to save you and now must keep it.

TRIPITAKA: Monkey, what is this bargain?

MONKEY: I am not allowed to say, Master.

TRIPITAKA: You have traded your life for mine, haven't you?

MONKEY: Please Master, I am not allowed to say.

TRIPITAKA: O Monkey, you are a foolish Monkey and I have grown so fond of you.

MONKEY: Please Master, remember, you are a monk, and I am a monkey.

TRIPITAKA: You know I would have gladly given my life to save yours.

MONKEY: Then you would not have succeeded in your quest and our journey would have been in vain.

SANDY: Brother Monkey, good-bye.

MONKEY: Good-bye, brother Sandy. Pigsy?

PIGSY: Stop it! Stop it! Good-byes always make me cry.

MONKEY: Good-bye Pigsy, my stupid friend.

TRIPITAKA: But Tathagata Father Buddha, is that it?

BUDDHA: Faith, Tripitaka, perhaps your story is not over yet.

*The Underworld.*

YAMA: Ah, you are welcome to the underworld, my monkey friend. These are my colleagues, the deathly demons.

A DEATHLY DEMON: Pleased to meet you.

YAMA: Ha-ha. I swore that I'd get you one day and I have, I've got you.

A DEATHLY DEMON: Your number's up this time.

A DEATHLY DEMON: His number's up once and for all.

Here it is, soul number 1350.

YAMA: Now, how shall I extract your soul from you?

MONKEY: Can you not just take it.

YAMA: O no. You cannot take a soul from a living being. The living being must die first. And since you have caused me such pain with all your tricks, I have thought of the most painful way of death for you.

A DEATHLY DEMON: What have you planned, Master?

A DEATHLY DEMON: What painful death have you planned for this malignant monkey?

YAMA: He shall be placed in a cauldron of boiling oil so that not only will his death be long and painful but we can feast on fried monkey parts when we have taken his soul.

A DEATHLY DEMON: You are a genius, Master.

A DEATHLY DEMON: An evil genius.

*A cauldron of boiling oil appears.*

YAMA: In you get Mr Monkey. Let's see whose books are cooking now.

*MONKEY gets in.*

What do you think you are doing you awful ape?

MONKEY: It was a long and dusty road to heaven. I'm having a bath. I call this transformation *Chill out Monkey.*

YAMA: You're not meant to have a bath, you're meant to die. Get him out of there! I've had enough of his games. I've had enough of his infernal games! Hold him down my deathly demons! There's only one thing left for it. His heart.

*YAMA pulls out MONKEY's heart. MONKEY dies. YAMA checks a few times. MONKEY does not move.*

I did it. I did it. He's dead. His soul is mine. Sun Wu-k'ung, the Monkey of the Mind is dead. Look!

A DEATHLY DEMON: Well done, Master.

A DEATHLY DEMON: You have won at last.

YAMA: Take this heart, put it in a paper bag and present it to that holy friend of his Tripitaka.

*TRIPITAKA, PIGSY and SANDY are flying home on a magic carpet. They crash.*

PIGSY: That double crossing, double dealing no good Buddha.

SANDY: I knew something like this would happen.

TRIPITAKA: Now we will never bring the scriptures to the Emperor of China.

*The noise of demons and monsters.*

SANDY: I've got a very bad feeling about this

PIGSY: I wish old Monkey was here. He always knew what to do.

*The sky darkens. The TWO DEATHLY DEMONS fly in.*

A DEATHLY DEMON: Someone here order some take away?

*THE DEMONS drop the bag which contains MON-KEY's heart onto the island and depart.*

PIGSY: What's this?

TRIPITAKA: I'm afraid Monkey is here, Pigsy. It's his heart. O my poor Monkey.

*All the DEMONS they have met along the way begin to circle.*

PIGSY: Monkey!

SANDY: Monkey!

TRIPITAKA: Monkey!

*The bag begins to beat.*

MONKEY: (*From the bag.*) Pigsy! My friends! It's time to play!

PIGSY: But Monkey, you're dead.

MONKEY: You can't kill Monkey, Monkey is irrepressible.

*MONKEY shoots through the bag and fights the DE-MONS. In the course of the fight, MONKEY, PIGSY and SANDY are knocked out. TRIPITAKA make the decision to fight. She fights and fights better than any of the other three who come to  as just she has finished. They congratulate each other.*

PRIME MINISTER: Emperor T'ai Tsang of the Empire of China, it is thirteen years and ten months since the monk Tripitaka, your sister, set off for the west. Surely she was killed or eaten along the way.

EMPEROR OF CHINA: I have not yet given up hope, Prime Minister.

PRIME MINISTER: But the bones of her guards were found years ago in the mountains.

EMPEROR OF CHINA: Enough, Prime Minister. I shall give her a few more days. She said she would return when that tree that faces west turns back towards the –

PRIME MINISTER: What is it Your Majesty?

EMPEROR OF CHINA: The tree.

PRIME MINISTER: What about it?

EMPEROR OF CHINA: It faces east. It faces east. Tripitaka, my sister is coming home.

*On a magic carpet, TRIPITAKA and her companions*

*arrive.*

Look! There she is. And see her friends carry the scriptures.

PRIME MINISTER: But they are ugly monsters.

PIGSY: 'We weren't born ugly just for the fun of it.' As the man says.

TRIPITAKA: Without my friends I never would have succeeded in my journey.

EMPEROR OF CHINA: They are welcome, as are you Tripitaka.

TRIPITAKA: Your Majesty, I have brought the scriptures from the Western Heaven. I am sorry that it took a bit longer than I expected.

EMPEROR OF CHINA: Do not apologise, Tripitaka, do not worry. You have achieved the impossible and what is time when we are talking about the impossible. Let me see these scrolls, Tripitaka.

*PIGSY and SANDY open them to show him.*

PIGSY: Here, Your Majesty.

TRIPITAKA: They contain all the laws that mankind needs to save himself from the sadness and afflictions of this life.

SANDY: But Master, there's nothing on them.

PIGSY: There's nothing written on any of them. That double-double-dealing low-down no-good Buddha.

TRIPITAKA: What? Was the whole journey in vain?

EMPEROR OF CHINA: May I see?

*They hold up the scrolls for the EMPEROR to see.*

No, there's something here. (*Reading.*)

In the beginning there was nothing
And nothing was everything;
The heavens, the air, the earth, the oceans and the under-
world
Were nowhere and everywhere;
For real form is that form which has no form
And Buddha's whole world is but a grain of sand.
Where true fullness is emptiness.

PIGSY: But what does that mean?

MONKEY: It means the journey was the message.

TRIPITAKA: And through the journey we have perfected
ourselves.

MONKEY: And on these scrolls must be written the story
of our journey.

TRIPITAKA: So others may follow on the path to enlightenment. We understand the meaning of this, Emperor.
Emperor?

*The EMPEROR stops reading. The scrolls are lowered.
The EMPEROR has trasformed into YAMA. Pause.*

MONKEY: We understand Buddha.

*YAMA transforms into BUDDHA.*

BUDDHA: I knew you would for you are all now Buddhas
too.

MONKEY: Well the one thing I don't understand, Father
Buddha, is since I too am now a Buddha, why do I have
to wear this headband to make me be good?

BUDDHA: Recite the prayer Tripitaka, everyone.

MONKEY: No! No!

ALL: Om Mane Padme Hum.

*Nothing happens to MONKEY.*

BUDDHA: The headband has been long gone, Monkey, you didn't notice. You didn't need it to be good, you only thought you did.

*All characters leave. MONKEY alone on stage.*

MONKEY: And so we all went home; Pigsy and Sandy to the Eastern Heaven, Tripitaka to Buddha, and Monkey to Flower-fruit Mountain, where it's always time to play.

*The End.*

# WWW.OBERONBOOKS.COM

Follow us on www.twitter.com/@oberonbooks
& www.facebook.com/oberonbook